The Span of a
Small Forever

The Span of a
Small Forever

Poems

April Gibson

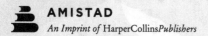
AMISTAD
An Imprint of HarperCollins*Publishers*

HarperCollins books may be purchased for educational, business, or sales promotional use. For information, please email the Special Markets Department at SPsales@harpercollins.com.

FIRST EDITION

Designed by THE COSMIC LION

Illustration by Net Vector/Shutterstock

Library of Congress Cataloging-in-Publication Data

Names: Gibson, April, author.
Title: The span of a small forever : poems / April Gibson.
Description: First edition. | New York : Amistad, 2024.
Identifiers: LCCN 2023031099 (print) | LCCN 2023031100 (ebook) |
  ISBN 9780063319172 (trade paperback) | ISBN 9780063319189 (ebook)
Subjects: LCGFT: Poetry.
Classification: LCC PS3607.I2645 S63 2024 (print) | LCC PS3607.I2645
  (ebook) | DDC 811/.6—dc23/eng/20231016
LC record available at https://lccn.loc.gov/2023031099
LC ebook record available at https://lccn.loc.gov/2023031100

24 25 26 27 28 LBC 5 4 3 2 1

For my boys, Greg and Jay.
My best work. My life's gift.

Contents

THE DRAPING OF BROODS

THE BLACK WOMAN PRESS CONFERENCE

The Span of a Small Forever

How to Survive Holding Your Breath

Recessive

I am the slim chance
auditioning
for my world premiere

The offbeat handclap
that will soon ruin the song

I am the shell game for which
you win a glitch

The enigma hiding inside
your insides

Riddle me this:

How many mistakes
does it take
to make a bad seed?

Transgression

As a child I didn't flinch at needles, didn't cry when I cracked my brow beneath grandma's cherrywood table playing hide-and-seek. The doctors tied me down to sew the stitches, applauded me for never moving an inch. My mother says they wanted to do a good job, to keep my face pretty. But vanity isn't what kept me still. It was my hidden talent of not knowing how to feel *feel*. For thrills I threaded safety pins through fingertips instead of playing Barbie dolls, dangled springy silver talons, warded off boys who thought themselves so strong and unafraid. They ran from me. I laughed at being left alone, roused at the empty gut, the deepness of it a blanket cut from lonesome craters on the moon, where I float and pluck stars like berries of glitter from endless black. A navigator of darkness, captain of agony, maybe that's what made the selection so natural—me—the chosen one to bear a suffering that would have surely taken my brothers and sisters away. They teased I was the favorite; suffice it to say I was special in the strangest of ways. I mean, I did love God most, even read his whole good book. By the time I was ten, I knew the story of Job, of the woman with the issue of blood, of women bowing and breaking and being made whole again. Perhaps it was my faith that called this ugliness into me, my fault for believing in miracles. Bludgeoned day by day from the inside out. A bodily offense turned sacrament.

Family History*

disease

can involve

different people

often spreads into the deeper layers of

life-

While there's no known cure

healing

people with

small

continuous

ease can

suddenly, without warning

include:

Reduced ▓▓▓▓▓▓▓▓▓▓ loss

▓▓▓▓▓▓▓▓▓▓▓▓▓▓▓▓▓▓▓▓▓▓▓

▓▓▓▓▓▓▓▓▓▓▓▓▓▓▓▓▓▓▓▓▓▓▓▓

Other ▓▓▓▓▓▓▓▓▓▓▓

People ▓▓▓▓▓▓▓▓▓▓▓▓▓▓▓ may ▓ experience:

▓▓▓▓▓▓▓▓▓▓▓▓▓▓▓▓▓▓

▓▓▓▓▓▓▓▓▓▓▓▓▓▓▓▓▓▓▓

▓▓▓▓ stones

▓▓▓▓▓▓▓▓▓▓▓

▓▓▓▓▓▓▓▓▓▓▓▓▓▓▓▓▓▓▓▓

When ▓▓▓▓▓▓▓▓▓

▓▓▓▓▓▓▓▓▓▓▓ you have persistent changes in your ▓▓▓

▓▓▓▓▓▓▓▓▓▓▓▓▓▓▓▓▓▓▓▓▓▓▓▓▓▓▓▓

▓▓▓▓▓▓▓▓

▓▓▓▓▓▓ pain

▓▓▓ in your ▓▓

▓▓▓▓▓▓▓

Ongoing bouts of ▓▓▓▓▓▓▓▓▓▓▓▓▓▓

▓▓▓▓▓▓▓▓▓▓▓▓

Unexplained ▓▓▓▓▓▓▓▓▓▓▓▓▓

▓▓▓▓▓▓▓▓ loss

▓▓▓

The exact cause ▓▓▓▓▓▓▓ remains unknown.

▓▓▓▓▓▓▓▓▓▓▓▓▓▓▓▓▓▓▓

▓▓▓▓▓▓▓▓▓▓▓▓▓▓▓▓▓▓▓▓▓▓

▓▓▓▓ Several factors, such as ▓▓▓▓▓▓▓▓▓▓

▓▓▓▓▓▓▓▓▓▓▓▓▓▓

██████████████████████████████████████

██████████████████████████████████████

████ a trigger. ████████████████████████

██████████████████████████████████████

██████████████████████████████████████

██████████ is more common in people who have family members with ██████████████████████████

██████████████████████████████████████

████████████████████ a ██████-history of ████████

Risk ████

████████████████████████████████████

████████████████████████████ at any age, but you're likely to develop the condition when you're young. ████████████████

██

████████

██████████ Although ██████ disease can affect any ██████ group████████████████████████████████████

████████████████████████████ ██████████, the incidence ██████████████ is increasing among Black people who live ██

████████████████████████ You're at higher risk if you have a first-degree relative ████████████████████████████ with ██ disease. ██

██

████████████████████

██

██

██████████████████████████████████

██

████████████████████████████████████

████████████████████████████████ While they do not cause

disease, they can lead to

Complications

obstruction.
Over time,
can scar and narrow

can lead to open sores
-anywhere in your mouth

can extend completely through
the -wall, creating an abnormal connection
between
you and your kin,

may bypass

between loops
causing continuous drainage of
your kin.
In some cases an
abscess, -can be life-threatening if not treated.
a small tear in
kin where infections can occur
often associated with painful movements may

make it difficult for you ▮▮▮▮▮▮ to absorb
enough ▮▮▮ to keep you nourished. ▮▮▮▮
▮▮▮

▮▮▮▮ Having ▮▮ disease ▮▮▮▮
▮ increases your risk of ▮▮▮▮▮
▮▮▮▮▮▮▮▮▮▮
▮▮▮▮▮▮▮▮▮▮
▮▮▮▮▮▮▮▮▮
▮▮▮

Other ▮▮ **problems** ▮▮ ▮▮▮▮▮▮
in other parts of the body. Among these ▮▮▮ are ▮▮▮
▮kin disorders, ▮▮▮▮▮▮▮
▮▮

▮▮▮▮▮▮▮▮▮▮
▮▮▮▮▮▮▮▮▮ associated with
▮▮▮▮▮▮▮▮▮▮
▮▮▮▮▮▮▮
▮▮▮▮▮▮▮▮
▮▮ fractures, ▮▮▮▮▮
▮▮▮ among other conditions. Work ▮▮▮▮ to
determine risks and benefits of ▮▮▮▮
Blood ▮▮▮▮▮▮▮▮▮
▮▮▮▮▮

*Erasure poem from Mayo Clinic's "Crohn's Disease" overview

Misdiagnosed

Half naked, cold, and bending I face the skinny glass
before they come circling the tight and too bright room.

I see a girl who isn't me, a girl who shouldn't be
a sack of bones crushing paper sheets to rustling white.

A white man in a white coat lifts my crumbling body
at the split, his hand barely touching what's left of it.

What's to see beyond the jutting ribs like mountains
caged beneath my flat and cardboard-colored chest?

He doesn't look me in the eye when a few minutes in,
the white man in the white coat traumatizes us again

with his diagnosis: he claims there is nothing wrong
with me, contends my ruined body a mere symptom

of what's been done to me, of what I've done to me,
or what I've done to it, what some would call a sin.

I know I can't be both a virgin *and* a whore. I mean,
I barely kissed a boy before, but who will believe me?

Even if my sick body doesn't match the sick crime,
the white man in the white coat has made up his mind.

All that's left is silence and quiet people in the room,
holding breath as they stare each other down and assume,

but the white coat never looks down, never sees
me looking up, as if to God, for answers to my agony.

My gaze extends beyond the pale into florescent white;
my body is a magic trick, disappearing me into the light.

With Every Fiber

I am a masquerader / anxious for gawking eyes to see /
beneath this slipping beauty, this disfigured heap / bound
by the nature of disease / said to be sprung from the dirt,
the gene—the world may never know / and it'd be too late
to matter: these tiny graves burrowing my body cannot be
undone. / *What more can I say of holes?* of wounds, of
tunneling fistulae of bloody stools, tears swimming drool /
of biting the bend in a corner of skin—a few seconds' reprieve
to numb the suffering. / *What more detail do you need?*
picture a girl drained to pale melanin, feigning normalcy /
squirming quietly in a hard seat / when a wail slips, it's
mistaken for the cackle of a happier child / not a girl
incessantly checking blue jeans for blemishes that reveal
her to be / akin to the sick woman with an issue of blood /
grabbing at His holy hem in anonymity / praying to be worthy
of a savior said to heal all wounds / but all that I touch turns
red as roses, like Midas gone awry / I am a wailing mound of
misery / twelve years clinging crumpled hands in hope / until
holy garments turn to white coats / prodding at this fissuring.

fistful of smeared sheets
each day is a white gown, soiled
open at the seam

A Change of Season

this one has a black box warning
but I don't really care, I am desperate
enough to inject the contents into flesh

        the vial reminds me of the movie
        Mission Impossible, a gadget that must
        be delivered on dry ice

the needles disappear
when I push down
for ten seconds

        hold breath
        months pass
        autumn ends

            the trial is over
            I didn't win
            a damn thing

I am not running and skipping
at picnics like middle-class
white people in the commercial ads

        I may be poor, but I am no less
        sick than the rich with this
        genetic glitch

my bones crackle, my skin
—a long road of rashes

        weeks of winter
        disappear like bubbles
        floating into thin air

                                    but I am still here
                                    stuck in this sheet
                                        crawling space

holding white wall corridors
bathroom floors on the days
my sons cannot bring me
sandwiches and juice

                        when they leave I shout
                        why me! to the empty house

I lie still
becoming a small stalk
in a windy field

                                held in a body
                                that will never be healed

Checklist

1. guzzle liters of colorless drink
2. wipe limbs in brown antiseptic
3. scrub iridescent nails with tiny alcohol pads
4. remove all jewelry
5. tuck loose curls into sky blue cap
6. bend shivering knees beneath pastel gown
7. clench teeth and chatter
8. try to recall your last meal
9. wake after nine hours of blank space
10. ask if any of this is real

Nil Per Os
(Post-Op Pantoum)

In the narrow bed, the curtain-split room
    everything is trudging the air around me
my hands move slowly toward my belly
    & feel the ways I have been carved apart

Trudging the air around
    I cradle the hole with nervous palms
I have been carved;
    listen to the emptiness, when I am less afraid

Cradle the hole, nervous
    look down: the protruding pink flesh stitched in
to the emptiness. I am afraid
    regretful permanency is all that's left

Stitched
    I watch the cleaning ladies sweep & mop
all that's left
    I wonder, will anyone come to wash me?

I watch ladies mop
    I have been left with just this one sponge
will anyone wash me?
    tiny, round & dusty as a piece of PAL gum

This one sponge
    stabbed with a stick of thin, pale wood
tiny, round
    I twirl it like an infinitesimal planet

Stabbed pale
    dip it in ice water held inside
an infinitesimal planet:
    the world's cup

Dip inside
    bring up for air, admire as if my own
world
    Ursa Minor, porous & peddling water

Bring up, admire as if my own
    mouth
Ursa Minor peddling water
    drops the count of jelly beans in a guess jar

Mouth
    ajar. a prize
the count of a guess
    roll unlucky sponge around pink wet

Ajar
    slip slowly out to paper cup. *Repeat*
sponge. pink wet
    do not swallow. *Repeat* until the sun

Slips slowly out. *Repeat*
    lift seafoam planet to orifice
swallow. *Repeat*. until
    dope heavy top to bottom

Lift planet to orifice
    clockwise my lips
top to bottom
    like a luscious stick of rouge

Clockwise my lips
    ice melts to lukewarm spit
a rouge
    dry crater in a flesh cheek

Lukewarm
    in the curtain-split room
my flesh a crater
        carved apart

How to survive holding your breath

Ninety pounds of skin draped over the bones.
An old lover would not recognize the me I see.
I do not want these scars or this strange body.
I want to wear a red bikini. I want a kiss on my belly.

For twenty-one days, the doctors come in swarms, hanging heads to pens unless speaking. My abdomen a crater sinking deeper with each labored breath. So many visitors, one could mistake my bed for a box. I can't remember all their names or even all the days it took to get here. But I do remember wearing lipstick when we passed the vomit days, and then there are the fuzzy images of my big sister tying big twists in my tangled hair. And the now-faint post-op screams from the epidural wearing off too soon.

For nine hours, surgeons cut away my sick parts, five hours beyond estimation. And the work remains undone. They explain my insides are too damaged, so they plan to continue the cutting next spring. Nevertheless, I am relieved that the hardest part is over. Being closer to "healthy" feels right, but somehow still feels strange. *Will I ever work the same? Will I ever again undress with pride?* My skin forever sticky with adhesive and the color of someone else's nude. I can never truly be naked again.

When I finally make it home, I cry at the sight of a tube top purchased the summer before. Staring down at my lifetime Band-Aid. This is what permanency feels like. On the right side of my belly, I carry the burden of desperation, the things we humans do to stay alive. I live in a time warp of constant repair—fixing. Never fixed. My body working through the darkness that knows to fill an empty space.

What is missing from me turns out to be more than ulcerated innards that span five feet. There is a displacement in me, a loss of the one constant my mind and body had for so long understood—a suffering. Though some may think what I mean to say is pain; I'm not sure these two words can translate the same. What I do know is that the first ten years of my life before being struck ill were filled with indoctrination that said suffering was a badge, an honor for the holy, a road to redemption from sin, a sign of great things to come, even if relief was to happen in the afterlife. Suffering is, then, by this logic, an oddly intimate act of faith, a response to pain. Pain, then, is a source of suffering, a feeling, a lonesome feeling, not an act but an affliction that when experienced creates an utter confusion of sense. A piercing touch can crumble you; the sound of your own child laughing can make you wince; the sight of blood, the smell of your own can make you puke; the metallic taste of medication can make you want to quit. But the promise of prayer, a response to suffering, can convince you to stay alive despite the pain.

But this is all semantics. To be honest, I just don't know what to do in this new body. Shameful to say, there are days I long for my missing pieces, some nights I want to rip this flimsy shield separating me from fragility and beg back the burden, welcome the suffering, accept the bad seed. Shame can feel stronger than love tries to be. And I'm not sure love will ever be enough to convince me I am worthy of the kind of life I see everyone around me take for granted.

My family assures me there are people who would want me even if I am not whole, though I can barely walk well enough to leave the house, let alone be concerned about how undesirable I have become. As I pace my small apartment half-dressed in a sports bra, my family pretends not to notice the scars. My six-year-old son is afraid of my new figure, confused about what will be my new toilet; he has developed an aversion to small plastic bags. He sees one from a local grocer with old tissues crumpled in a kitchen corner and nervously picks it up when I tell him to toss it in the can. Only my niece is bold enough to ask why my body is different. I answer in truthfulness because children need to understand that people sometimes live with holes inside themselves, real holes or holes that only they can feel.

My nephew calls me an alien, weird but supercool. I laugh and let my hands tell the story, making gestures with the scientific words. They all gather in a circle and listen. They want to touch me. I let them touch me. Then there is awe and question. Searching for shame in the lines of my face, they find none. They look at their own bellies. The girl excitedly shouts how we are the same: small brown fingers pointing to tiny nicks in her skin.

An Awkward Ode to My Awesome Stoma

my peekaboo belly worm
    warm-blooded body snake
stalking my stain of a story
    the nerve of you
making holes in me
    my fishing hook
emptying pink mess
    pulled through flesh
my Jesus side wound
    my Sisyphus
why must you make a fool of me?
    my disconnected regret
low-hanging pink pet
    red sunset: the dawn
beneath my shirt
    bloody tangle
my misdirected snout
    my body's new way out
gargling spout
    belly-mouth tongue out
you love me so much
    you choke when I swallow
breathe when I drink
    my wet noisemaker
my skinned elephant trunk
    geyser carrying my dirty

stream, wilted rose
    my weepy willow
blood at the roots
    my glossy gut stem
broken, but not like bone
    a kind mistake
in my landscape:
    you may not be a charming flaw
    like a cute dimple or mole
    but you are my magical hole
    keeping all that is in me *whole*

Vestiges

Baptism

Face beneath a wash rag, he dunks me quickly in a large swimming pool. I am only five and already made anew. We have church in storefronts and hotel conference rooms, from the Westside to Downtown. The Saints sing, praise, and worship invisible things. The gifted speak in distant tongues. I force a hard roll inside my mouth some Sundays, but the heaven mumble never falls out, so I crawl under a back row of chairs with seats the color of puke and play with the other littles, waiting for the after-sermon sermons to end. Since Daddy is the preacher man, we have Bible study on Wednesday nights in our home filled with books, stacked along the wall, in messy corners, citing the importance of the one and only Jesus Christ. I read Holy Scriptures front to back. Recite them to impress. Though my imagination can sometimes run amok, making Revelation a bedtime story, frightening little brothers in a dim attic bedroom, learning to bring damnation to life.

***

Biology proves that a curved bone was never enough to create a woman. Turns out school is not a place for testaments of shaping the whole world in a solitary week. Something inside me wants to stop listening to fathers and gods. But something else in me still loves Sundays, the day my father takes a long bath or opts to soak in musky cologne, the day he wears colorful, shiny shoes and instructs me to iron his shirt; fumes of man fan with the steam. The day I wake early to hear him preach on the radio, later hearing the same message at church, where my siblings and I will spend half the day playing with cousins, laid across a back row of metal and mauve seats, sleeping in a slouch on top. When the drag-out speech of Black tradition subsides, I will beg my father for crumpled dollars in front of other people, because this way he will not say no. These *God* days I am more than a quiet girl with a scowl who never wears name-brand shoes or pierced earrings. On Sundays I am not alone in a corner with books, not being an outcast of the tribe. I am part of bigger things like universe and the beginning of time. God is a reason to keep my feet from floating between shards of stars, in outer-space places, where I think the heavens hang.

Ruins

In the silence of starless sky
    he folds night into a vestige,
threading visions of the past
    memory filling with a blond
inculcated lie, rendering white
    Jesus a thorn festering inside,
leaving mine an unhealed head
    to balance, to realign these relics
on repeat: a ceaseless savior
    who feasts on unrequited prayer
was fed incessantly to me;
    my luck, my dreams, my being
beyond a world of free will
    even after the red pill, seems
still his choice to make
    my mind like the wafer snapped
in two, is too his to bend, to break.

The First Book of Escape

I once feared my fate after death
2 A girl obsessed with Rapture
being left behind, filled my mind
each night, a fatalistic scene
3¶Dark cavities gobbled into
Earth's bedrock, chock-full of
bodies broken and mended,
on repeat
4 Transgressors of a malevolent
God, damning his own creations
as gifts for demons to torment
5¶Strange, when you think
about it
6 I thought about it a lot

7 Years of pulling back the
curtain exposed the afterlife
to be
8 Little more than a mirror
9¶A fun-house mirror,
you see
10 Shiny devils telling lies
11 Flawed revelations between
fractures desperate for the light
12¶A sight that leaves you
scratching
13 Searching thine own eyes
for beams
14 For that speck you'll never see

Notes from a visit to the Mütter Museum

They say *no photos*, so I commit images to memory.
The exhibit named *Imperfecta* unveils the vestiges
of human err, a catalogue of antiquity's eyesores,
genetic defects misunderstood as the devil's work
or a father's bad seed taken on as a mother's curse.
Blasphemies encased in airtight glass, yellowing pages
of medieval text reveal woodcuttings of fetal positions.
I study the drawings, the way the unborn is repeatedly
sketched as a small madman making the womb look like
a tight and tiny hell. Embalmed fetuses lie on display,
spectacles of three legs or splayed backs. A French 16th
century surgeon lists the thirteen causes of monsters,
of which the foremost is glory of God. Worn documents
philosophize the sublime, declare it is formed with equal
parts admonishment, fascination, and terror. I imagine
how easy it must have been to see innocent babies
as jinxed, wicked beings before a concept of childhood
came to exist. When I leave the physicians museum
I am left wondering who and what do we mis-identify
and leave for dead in these times, for our lack of vision.

Vestiges

black holes tunnel a Milky Way through my body   my belly fills

    again with a blond and bearded god   even in the deep space

of imagination   white Jesus is a thorn in my mind

    what an unhealed head I balance

religious relics on repeat   claiming the only road to harmony

                      .   is someone else's savior
your luck his choice to make

          your body like the wafer snapped in two

is, too, his to bend & break

          I grew up haunted

             by God's omnipotent eye

his face pressed against

            the cold side of a bedroom window
listening

for wicked fantasies as I slept

his reflection in glass blocks

          on the nameless church across the street

God lived in the beep of a dial tone

          the end & the alpha of all things

everything was penance

       a lesson to forgo joy

        as the path to forgiveness

all for the sins of a naked man & woman eating apples in the grass

New World

Theft is invisible to the West
& shame nowhere to be found
      on this map & ugly city
      paradise littered with
broken redwoods, brown cones
tumbling roads from LA to
      Oakland to San
      Francisco Bay, yellow
currents with golden alchemy,
where even the gudgeon refuse
      the hook, pulling life
      out of everything in sight,
the condor watching, waiting
for the fall of the West
      & the rest   & the best
      & the wall came tumbling
down down baby
down the rollercoaster
      sweet sweet girls singing,
      jumping, barrettes
smacking faces & backs
trapped in the double Dutch
      rope, as the sun sweats
      its glow to a puddle of lava
rolling slowly toward the water
where the yachts begin to sink

down down the city, twisting,
turning upon itself putting
Dali's stroke to shame,
sweet sweet baby
just because I kiss you
don't mean I love you

Dawn

We confused our own treachery
with mad science conspiracies,
pandemics, and poisonous air.
Something or someone
all-seeing and never seen
in a cloud of abhorrence
will eat our shadows, in time.
With no aid from Armageddon
leaving little for the zombies, it
watches as we gnaw our own apart,
explode the rest to smithereens
in celebratory fashion, as would all
creatures of decay, all species of
transmutable beasts, with enough
supremacy to survive ourselves
alone, in a world that will never be
new, no origin in a fiery sky,
no unveiling in an ocean tomb.
In this dirt is where we shall stay,
crawling on our wet, ugly bones,
forever amending histories
that do not want us anymore.

Re-memory

Superstar

sitting sideways in the green velvet chair
I hear him sing, *a chair is still a chair /*
even when there's no one / sitting there
my mind goes in circles, spinning hair

greasing Grandma's fingers to endless
plaits, on Sunday after days of picking
parts at the plastics factory, she presses
my curls, after scrubbing and soaking

I shine like polished stars before the dawn
she pours coffee black as tar, woos and fawns
while cooking sausage, split flat and crispy
the eggs fried hard, the rice sweet and sticky

floral drapes thin the sunlight, breeze zooms
teeth combing clouds of cumulous kink
carrying tunes to a room that *is* a room
doo doo doo doo doo floats the air then sinks

cushions of yellow high-back chairs, nearby
brown encyclopedias multiply
mirror over mantel décor: one set
tureen, matching mugs, German castles etched

blades of grass cut to obedient blocks
guard this brick bungalow that *is* a home

out back Grandpa reveals fragments flocked
North toward a new kind of "Up South" home

aside garage, tomatoes grow. I pick
a red one, listening to Johnnie preach
'bout these last two dollars, as blue notes lick
and Grandpa sings along, shuffling his feet

cords crack the smoke of BBQ ribs, hot
red links, charred and stuffed slit a flimsy bun
I bite, balance bent crown stuck in a knot
atop cramped curtsy in kitchen chair, spun

coils twisting, trying not to shed a tear
Grandma pulls tightly the last dark tendril
of hair, piano plays *so sweet and clear*
his voice sounds close enough to almost feel

'til the song skips, ending Luther's live show
reminding me . . . *it's just the radio*

An Homage to Latchkey Kids

They dig for treasures deep in the couch, unearth coins in muddy cracks of concrete, all for a chance to spend pennies on sweets—*frooties* stick and bury their soon-to-rot teeth; Black girls in *white girls* with gum-speckled soles skip city sidewalks and dash in the wind, gripping warm bags of chips with cheese and beef; they scurry and eat ghetto snacks in the street; the biggest girl twirls, revealing a key tied to a string Hula-Hooping her neck; *if you lose it, we gone be locked out!* the baby girl shouts, but there's always a way to squeeze through the back, even if by the hair of their chins; they meet up with friends, opt out the 3:30 fight with rough girls from around the way; no time for windmill punches anyway; the sun is falling away; they rush with flung backpacks, noses running fast as their feet; fingers laced beneath the dusk, a dingy constellation of three, bursting open the front door, fighting to embrace their mother who skipped overtime today; excitedly they zip past strewn figurines, past Daddy stepping atop Wolverine, yelling at brothers as they bark and howl; the night crowds the window, revealing a fog of moths fluttering in flight as the streetlights ignite.

Up South

A block of brick bungalows, symmetric lawns, porches
and concrete steps filled with Black families who proudly
walked in the front door as white people ran out the back.

A house so beautiful, people and roaches never wanted to leave.
The place to be: basement parties, purple lights, lace gloves,
costumes trimmed in gold and glitter; it was the '80s after all.

One room covered in strawberry shortcake décor, canopy bed
in pink, and of course there are the makeshift rooms: a pantry
just big enough for a crib, but the little girl leaves each night

to crawl into her sister's bed because the thick white plastic
mattress is too loud; it makes her think of that bout with
chicken pox, the explosion of scratched blisters against

the sound of her bed's flammable coat; back then anything
could catch fire—pajamas, hair, even people smoking dope;
if you were quiet enough you could find lessons in loud things:

loud people, loud music, and even in the smoke; the hot, rattling
speaker thumping bass across the street, the screech of Mama
singing Prince at the top her lungs in the red-light gathering

a floor beneath; the scratch of a record, which you learn
is on purpose; the cloud of white dust swirling heads
like an extra layer of holding spray; if you could be seen

and not heard, you'd learn why they call a drum a heartbeat, what make the bass go boom, why the beat make folks wanna do "the butt," and you'd learn how to be sexy when you grow up.

Love is

Lying in your mother's lap, sitting between your grandma's knees, as she stuffs your too-short bang into a pink plastic roller. Love is your big sister teaching you to do your baby hair so you can look like Chilli from TLC. Love is crazy, sexy, *and* cool. Love is learning a recipe for peach cobbler by watching, with the only record of instruction being *"do it to taste."* Love is listening. Speaking up. Shutting the fuck up even if you're right. Love is warning your little brother not to dance on a barstool, him doing it anyway, seeing his elbow break the fall, setting his broken bones until Mama makes it home from work. Love is *"fall back and let me catch you."* Watching your mother dance to Prince all night. Gleefully dancing by yourself in the mirror at midnight, naked and alone, running your fingers along pulled stretches of skin spread across your thighs. Love is growing a stranger inside your body, feeding him the watery milk of your breasts with cracked nipples, burning the soft side of your wrist to test a bottle's temp. Love is being hungry and giving your child the last piece. Love is watching old Black movies with your sons, spilling crumbs in the sheets, cackling and giggling. Love is what my father *meant* to offer when he sang to me as a baby, *"That's my little cutie-pie / and everybody wanna know why she cry."* Love is him meaning to hold on and not let go. Love is knowing when to let go. Love is honoring the living and the dead. Giving praise to Black Jesus, even when you are unsure of why, because this makes your family happy and you less heathen-like. Love is my great-grandmother pointing at my ten-year-old body, demanding, *"If a man ever touch you there, tell me,"* signaling because there are no words for some things, or at least shouldn't be. There is no word for *like* in some languages, only *love*. And love is not the opposite of hate. Love is not having to compromise and compromising anyway. Being terrified and doing it anyway. Sometimes love is not the showing-up; it is the staying. Kissing a scar formed from a wound you didn't heal or create. Love is watching a lover's hip become a hill to climb. The smell of an exhale after a kiss. Love is singing along to "Sweetest Taboo," staring eye to eye after the rain, wondering why the rain keeps the grass growing, why the grass keeps the bugs fed, why bugs keep the birds full. The way the birds remind us to wake up, to look up, is a kind of love. Love is a choice and a destiny, instinctive and insane, humble and courageous, of body and mind. Love is the closest thing to travelling time.

Brown Girl Merry-Go-Round

A brown girl sits outside a brown door. The smell of stale cigarettes lingers the hall. A woman celebrated for her quaintly decorated, clean and fragrant spaces, despite fumes from the hoagie shop below, is inside. *A brown girl waits outside a brown door.* It is Friday again, payday again, and Daddy comes home being somebody else again. Smoke floats behind her flat chest, but she's not holding her breath for an end to weekend battles that only circle back, like the white rings of smoke she puckers as she waits outside, listening to the same two fists, same couch scratching same wall. *A brown girl stands outside a brown door.* She watches the same two cops come down the hall and take him away for the calm-down-don't-kill-her round-the-block ride, but he still leaves with the check, lost and off searching for something in whiskey and tramps. Momma stays. Momma cries. Momma finds another way to eat. *A brown girl goes inside a brown door.*

Bad like Jesse James

In alley they gather like clouds of carried-on Mississippi
cackling baritone tongues droning on 'bout these last two
dollas & who they strokin' on; the stereo collects the beat
dust of a house rug; Top Cat, Bubba & crew settle two
white buckets, one folding chair, an orange milk crate
leaning back against the chain-link fence, gripping sweaty
cans of MGD; the pack face the tracks as commuter trains
rush by, blown horn drowning their leader howling from
beneath the brim of what could have been a Dobbs hat,
but he was more bearer of Afro donned in a mesh-back
snap cap; Top Cat never sported the ornaments of pimps,
though Baby Girl crowns him ruler of an unseen dynasty
diamond in the back joint; her juke & switchblade hero,
his whiskey halo charming womens wall-to-wall deep,
thick candy-red grins never smiling sweet & striking
as his gapped-tooth wife be, when she be
yelling for him to bring his ass in the house.

Coldwater

for Madea

We pile into the rented minivan, more people than seats. Set out for our customary voyage back to sweltering Mississippi, a summer "vacation" every Black child Up South would take. We eat cold cuts and cheese product sliced, quartered, packed back into the bag. Children cramp unbuckled on the floor, scarfing down "sweat sandwiches." We stop for gas and piss breaks at stations where we see women climbing in and out of semitrucks. Grandma demands we not enter the restroom alone. After half a day's drive south, we make it to the town of Coldwater. The place where my mother was born of a dry birth on a couch in her grandmother's house. My great-grandmother Dewdrop stands waiting at the door. The smell of fresh biscuits swirls the air around her head-rag hair. And the memory stops there: the romanticizing of a South I never had to live in. One I stopped visiting after enough people died and the funerals became further apart. This homemade recollection is not the part of my great-grandmother that stayed. It was instead the lessons on land and how not to lose it. The frankness about men and how to tell on them if they touched me wrong. How being smart meant that you could clean a house well. How she cleaned white women's houses once upon a time. How there was a story about her being called a monkey and brazenly flashing her ass to prove to a white child she did not, in fact, have a tail. The way we laughed when she told us, "You can't talk to white folks like that," whenever we did things like complain about service. How I realized later, for her, it wasn't a joke. How she said "did" in so many inflections, she could articulate every emotion in three letters. How later I learned the meaning of prescriptive grammar. How she didn't go through much school, but she could read and write. How I keep the handwritten letters she wrote me with all kinds of subversive, simple advice, telling me things like, "Know everybody smile at you not your friends, just be aware of that, just keep't'awalking." How I wrote back and keep writing because so much has been erased. How no matter what story I tell, everything always comes back to the water.

Location. Location! Location?

My sister calls to frantically tell me of a cotton field in North Carolina, having never experienced such a sight before, and how she refused to touch the bolls of Gossypium because she felt stalked with an almost laughable yet deeply rooted fear of being snatched back into slavery.

How do we come to know so well the places we have never been? How do we sense where we should or should not be? When the place from which you come has no past to locate, but *is* and *be*, how do you leave it behind?

The possibility that our freedom is a fleeting reality, or not a reality at all, is a cultural trauma that hunts. History, for us, is not a fossil. It breathes. It is alive. Every day scratching our backs, beading a sticky sweat upon our skin.

Migrations

for Ernest J. Gaines

Ashen soles marched the gravel,
    the peaks, down the valleys
    over the hills, through bridgeless waters
We waded
    the fields and fog of swamps, from tail end
    to mouth of river
We walked
    with babies on backs or left back behind,
    sent ahead sometimes
We met halfway
    other times we never made the meeting
We walked
    with big-lipped shoes, boots with no straps,
    nothing to pull for
Walked
    away with strange homelands tucked in
    the curl of toes, sore crack of heels
We never forgot to kneel
    above the dirt, beneath the sky of some kind
    of necessary God
Walked
    through the sticky mouth
    of summer, noticed the hummingbird,
    its honeysuckle, tickled a callus 'cross
    blades of grass

We cradled
    earth against a blister,
    let it lull the whites of feet
We made it on our own two feet
    with tired hands yielding
    little fruit for our own salivation,
    harvesters with no harvest,
    bent-bodied salvation
Walking North
    into the wind
    of autumn filled with the fragrance
    of burnt wood and wet leaves
    until
We reached the smoke:
    our own breath in winter, fiery limbs
    wavering in the cold, gray sky

Blue Magic

(at Silver Lake, St. Anthony, Minnesota)

If I stare long enough
    anything can look like home
A drooping tree can be
    my grandmother's green
drapes, the thick, heavy ones
    popular in the 70s
The poplar tree can be
    the thing that stole away
my granddaddy and that
    house he never built
A blade of grass—the butcher
    knife used for family dinners
A twig—the wooden handle
    pressing splinters into palm
Scratching squirrels—the bent
    fingers of my sister's hand
oiling my dry scalp
    The mud—*Blue Magic*
Weeds—the rat-tail end of a comb
    Sparrows—neighbor kids
tapping pebbles on the glass
    asking in a high-pitched whisper
Can y'all come out and play?
    Crows—their raucous parents
who fight every other day
    while ants play the part

of kitchen roaches, scattering
    beneath my feet
as I stand at the pond's edge
    A crawling breeze becomes
the hemline of my mother's dress
    sweeping a fragrance of gentleness
If tenderness could have a smell
    it would be sweet as the pinkish
wet of sliced watermelon
    before drying to a drip
at my elbow's tip, sweet as the blue
    bottom of a Firecracker Popsicle
inking the center of my pink tongue
    If I stand still long enough
I can feel the sun of my youth
    like the warmth of a gas bill paid
on a Midwest winter's day
    But *today*
I welcome summer's shade
    in a world of new surrounding blue
as if this is a place where I belong

The Draping
of Broods

Neighborhood Watch
(South Side, Chicago. Afternoon.)

I.

Look at *her*!　　　　　　knees like jelly

　　　　she know *damn* well　　them heels too high

'Bout like to break her ashy ankles

　　　　　　　　　　in them cheap street-walking shoes

Poor child　　　got the shape of a woman already

　　　　Ain't even have a chance　　once she hit the block

Listen at them,　　　　crazy fools yelling

　　　　　　　from porches and corners and car windows

Whistling　　ringing like alarms　　shouting nasty words

　　　　for every bone　　　　in that child body

Look at her　　　pulling at the hem

　　　　　　　　like *that's* gone make the skirt grow back

They likely to rip it off her　　men ain't got no *damn* sense!

Like *wild* animals I tell you . . . damn shame.

Don't *you ever* walk out this house looking fast like *that*

             You hear me?   (commercial ends)

Honest to God, it's her mama fault
                         her mama a crackhead

But that's her *mama*   only God got right to correct

                                             Ain't my place

                                                (game show begins)

What child services gone do?

                             she be worse off than before

                                             Everybody hands tied

And I ain't never been the kind to get in nobody's business

             But I *heard* the drug man buy that girl

                                 from her mama sometimes

Trick her out to groups of men

                 men know they some *nasty* dogs

Damn shame how *drugs* is ruining the community

(she backs up from the window)

Hell the police gone do?

they ain't never done no good

Everybodyhandstied

What a shame

I *heard* that girl got the other girl from down the street

in them streets too

Nothing but skin and bones

ain't even got *nothing* to look at

But they done got *real* fast now:

switching on the block late at night

Riding round in fancy cars always in some new clothes

shame can't nobody *do* nothing though

You know how teenage girls be smelling *y'all self* and all

Everybody.   Hands.   Tied.

(she puts her hand on her hip)

Didn't I *tell* you already it's her *mama* fault

the girl don't know no better

She wasn't raised right

a bad woman can't make a girl act right

Anyway, ain't none of that my place

only business I got is to teach *you* better

Cuz *you* ain't like them *fast-tailed girls*   You better

You a *good* girl who was raised *right*   remember that, *all right?*

Neighborhood Watch II

She puts her bra on headfirst, wrestles
cotton triangles speckled with polka dots
across her flat chest, rubs Teen Spirit into
hairless pits, steps into panties with blue
letters spelling *Wednesday*; today, she will
wear those new clothes—a gift from the man
who drives the fancy car; she slicks hair back,
wraps a white, a red, a blue scrunchy round
strands in a twisted knot, turns rhinestones
in circles, loosens crust gathered in the lobe,
rolls cherry Lip Smacker counterclockwise:
her mouth mimics the mouth of a fish; gold
polish on nails shaped like quarters of moon;
one hand neat, the other unsteady; sparkles
spill outside the lines; outside the horn is
blowing; she bites away what's left of white
tips, inhales the chemical smell, exhales
and counts backward from three,

> Mississippi . . .

cool breath blown 'cross fingers;
the man in the fancy car blows harder

> two, Mississippi . . .

she shoves her feet into a pair of chunky black
Mary Janes, as knees wobble like Jell-O;
her fingers tremble, and glitter twinkles
like wet lights collapsing inside her
sweaty palms folding to fists

> one, Mississippi . . .

Ghazal for a Fast Black Girl
Gazing from a Locked Window

My parents left my ballooning body in a small town filled with white
pro-lifers, a man-made lake, room & board, food labels black-and-white.

I am fed food-pantry goulash and buckeye confections on football days.
Taught catch-up credits by volunteers who look like nuns—old and white.

There are other lessons too, like God being first, then man, then woman,
and how the ills of Eve live on in fast girls like me, who are not white.

They convince me the Devil is real. I cannot leave this hell, save for church.
This place is an almost convent for Evangelicals (the ones who are white).

I am not a nun-in-training, and I do not love God as much as people say
I should. Besides, in most religion, God becomes a man who is white.

No matter the faith, I would still be unworthy and full of sin; I want to ask
the mad-mother-hen, *How long does it take to be good if you are not white?*

They say Jesus forgave even the worst of people. *Am I worse than all of these?*
What a waste of time trying to change the minds of Christians who are white.

I save important questions for "doctor" visits with a plump pink midwife,
blond bangs swaying as she checks my pink cervix with fingers that are white.

She chuckles at my fears for getting this mistake in my young body out.
Assures I needn't worry, for Black skin can stretch further than the white.

She smirks as if having offered a gift, her signaling thumb and longest digit pressed into a colorless pinch, parted to flushing tips, then back to white.

I feel like an invisible object pulled in two, viscous as the peanut butter insides of old buckeyes stuck in the bottom of my belly, which is not white.

I almost believe them when they say I don't deserve my almost child, that they deserve my seed more, even if Black babies are never first pick for the whites.

In the end, I have no choice in the matter, for other methods would land me in the bottom circle of hell. *Remember, April,* the devil is real (and white).

Domesticated

I live in her bed for six weeks
my mother helps me learn quickly

the blanket wrap: diamond-angle
-angle-tip-tuck-pull tight

to use the soft side of wrists
to grease an areola's dry split

she takes Polaroid pictures
of a pose on repeat

her words like parallelograms
in blue ink

scripting blank white into memory
each smile one thousand elegies

every tomorrow yesterday's rerun
warm bottles, their nipples, my own

milk and a stranger's vomit
shit in tight-knot plastic bags

I am a machine girl, wiping gently
the face, patting softly the back

feeding god's poked hole in the night
a weeping ball of tissue, crusting new

nail beds traced in brown half-moons
fingers clawing themselves to fists

oil between my hands and his
—nothing on the inside.

The Draping of Broods

I.

I think the bed has plastic over the mattress, not sure, but it is
small and uncomfortable. There are three rooms and, at first, six
girls. They put me with the other Black girl in a small room on
the left side of the hall, chilly at night with the smallest closet,
not as bright as the other two rooms. The sun hides from this
side of a house that used to be some kind of hospital. There are
alarms on the windows, as if stick figures harboring humanity
will escape through rectangles with a pair of those cheap,
donated sheets and scale the brick, or maybe we will sew the
towels together after we unravel them from obediently folded
positions—rolled the same way every time, no creases on top.
Except, we cannot sew, cook, clean, or do anything good and
right. We can only be six girls with no honor, on a second floor
funded by "the saints," where we make goulash, wash dishes,
go to grocery stores and church in a thirteen-passenger van
like a small band of scarlet whores, madwoman-missionary at
all times by our side. We make calls on weekends, if there is
anyone left to listen. All mail prescreened; love letters tossed.
Sometimes visitors, but mostly not; live visits are watched
closely by the minister-madwoman-mother-god on the first
floor. Twice in 120 days, my family remembers I am not home.
They visit me, stay for dinner. We take a photo. My littlest
brother touches my belly as we pose. They drive off and leave
me once again with the mad-woman-mother-hen beneath
checking for the swiftness in twelve steps above.

Mother hen is with us on two when the first baby dies, when
we watch the other Black girl struggle down the poorly lit hall,
crawling the walls. There is a rush, then a calm, and the pink
matter begins to unswim her. She thinks it was a boy, so we say
he had her feet, though really it has no feet at all, only webs
with tiny slits, but if we squint, we tell her we can see a toe.
Birthing a dying thing is like having god strike you from the
inside out, like cutting your hair before it grows, digging flat
follicles with blades, razoring roots in a frantic part-and-peel.
She wants to grow wings, rocket through the dropped ceiling,
and strike god back. Her emblem—a badge of dishonor—
stitched across her stiff breasts filled with unusable milk. She
swings skinny arms at the air, feet still on the ground, fighting
the sky as the madwoman drapes her buckling brown body in a
bedsheet cape.

II.

In my grandmother's bathroom of absolute coordination and
immaculate floors, I am trapped on the blue toilet, making a
nest of palms, as if catching a small river will keep the ocean
inside from spilling out. Frantically I call her to the door. She
calls *him*, and he shows up in someone else's car. I journey
on my back, spread across the seat like a whale preparing to
spray. The dark sky is blurred with streetlights and the lineage
of moths. On this night in the middle of January, the city is
motionless, but my body is moving too fast. This baby belongs
to St. Valentine, and I know something is wrong. I feel tiny
fists in my body trying to squeeze and claw all that is in me out.
When I reach the hospital, they won't let me shut my thighs.

The nurse's hand occupies the space between. She will not take her hand out my pushing place. Something is *wrong*. "Yes, Miss, something *is* wrong." Her hand is holding the cord so he won't die, so my body won't kill him. This boy, who will only grow to be a man like *him*. Her hand still stuck into me. There will be no pushing. The room is ready. This will be an unnatural birth. They will cut him from my belly. They will give me scars. They will cut and stab into me. I secretly hope they stab me wrong, so he will die. I want to scream to them:

> *Give this baby back to god!*
> *I don't know what to do with life!*
> *I lied. I surrender. Please, just*
> *give him back to god!*

But the words stay trapped in my belly with the boy.
God gives him to me.
I stare at the tiny, naked stranger held above the hole in me.
Hear a doctor's work praised for its precision.
See a smiling nurse declare I can still wear a bikini.

> Then everything goes black.

***

It's the second day, and I'm still high. I see colorful oblong people who smile crookedly when they say *congratulations*. Where is the boy? Where is yesterday?

On the second night I beg them not to leave this baby here, but they leave this baby here. And I do what I am told with my breasts. Become a breathing food supply filled with colostrum and ache, clicking a high-dose drip to the max until I pass out

with the boy. I wake in a reflex as he rolls from my breast, down
my arm, to my hand, the floor wants to steal his brains
                     but, I catch his tiny body
                              but I catch his tiny body!
                                        I save him!
                                        I save *my son*.

My son, the Capricorn
who one night before
    defeated his own death.   I saved him.
                                    And now I want another
                                    chance to love him back.

Tête-à-tête
for Gregory

My lips formed in the shape of train smoke
half-moons and wet kisses

I taught you how to use your own
from suckling to sovereignty

you grew to a sky cracked open
you became a thundercloud

I remained a tulip tree, giant but pendulous
littering yellow flowers about the earth

as your words trembled my roots in a way
that is not the shaky stutter of small things

storms were created to tell us the story of sound
how it began as silence and formed a tongue

lips, teeth, then ears to hear the making
of its own noise, and become its own voice

My Boys

Last night, I watched without remark or too long a stare, my sons randomly slip into a dance routine that seemed natural, in sync, freestyled and full of joy. Do you know how amazing it is to see your two brown boys share in delight, especially when one is like a man and the other praying for muscles, how heartwarming it is to see the little one follow the speed of his big brother until his little frame burst with laughter at how fast they are turning round and round, to peek at them sliding left and right across the floor, making their limbs into a geometry only brothers could ask and answer? At this moment, I realize they have always done this, had this, with or without me. I realize how important it is for me to understand—I am not the key to my children's happiness, but they know how to create it, shape it, how to make it all by themselves.

Queen Maker

Dirty corners, crumbling partitions once white
baseboards fragranced in nomad piss, sullied
as newborn cries drowned out by loud speakers
muffling mismatch names, calling me out
and away from the stares of a chubby Mexican
toddler running free through these makeshift
aisles of hard plastic seats, his orange shirt
stained with grease, squeezing his small belly,
his face swelling with exasperation and smeared
spit, as fingertips examine our memoirs in manilla
envelopes, stuffed by overworked, ashy hands
inking our lives in the folds of paid postage.

By the time I make it to the back, he is laid flat
on the dusty laminate. I pose no questions to
the inquiries: the right answer is what they say
it is. What they say it is can fill a family of bellies,
rotting teeth, a house with heat, and worry with
some kind of rest. No matter how right, it is
not wise to fight a battle that can only be won
if your babies can't eat, cuz if your babies can't eat,
none of this shit matters. Remember, sometimes
holding fists too high will only make hands heavy.

I keep mine open. I survive today.

3x5 Ekphrasis of a Past Life

My hands fish memories in a plastic bin of things I wish to dump into an ocean. There are beautiful flowers behind our backs. The grass is green, shutters white and neat. And I am smiling with arms bent at your shoulders, my limbs still thick from the thirty pounds of "baby fat" I gained mostly in the shape of uncomfortable breasts, ballooned from random cravings for ramen noodles, peanut butter and jelly, and Cap'n Crunch berries. I had the baby too soon. But when I healed from the cuts in my womb, I ran to you, living together in the finished basement of a split-level suburban house, beneath your mother's footsteps. My feet were always cold on the brown tile floor, your breath always heating my ears with mean words and cruel laughter. I remember often wanting to kill you in your sleep. You hold him in your right hand. I wear your mother's pearls, looking almost old enough to drink. I wear my hair the same as girl me, parted on one side, slick with gel, jet-black. It is still thin on the left from those pulling years. The boy is smaller than he should be, five pounds of pale smudge, dark suckling lips. You are smaller than the last day I saw you, your face less round, your body underdressed in jogging pants and a wrinkled tee. I must have gone somewhere without you, though your mother always teased that you'd lock me in a closet if you had your way. Never the boy I wrote about in diaries or cut from magazines. You were ordinary. And I was more than the lies you told me about myself. Sometimes, you think you need a person, then he, she, or the love they won't give just doesn't matter anymore.

Somebody else shows up, or maybe never left. You love yourself anyway, or maybe never stopped. The Earth keeps spinning on its axis, gravity still works, and so do your feet. There are things only film can make real. Everything looks better when we're standing still.

9/11, selective amnesia, and banana cookies

Yesterday my son turned twenty-two. I remember the year he was born, him being tiny, wobbly with a head too big for his body. But when I push the memory, I end up thinking of 9/11, which happened when he was nine months old. I was leaning against a couch in my grandmother's basement that had been converted into a daycare as my son crawled across a rug with race cars and roads in front of the television, everyone watching images of planes crash into skyscrapers over and over again.

Not sure why these images stick out most about the first year of my first child's life. There were so many other things to remember. I'm sure. But I was seventeen, suffocating in a toxic relationship with a man who I see twenty-two years later as no more than a . . . I don't really wanna talk about that. I don't wanna talk about him, about the person who choked me literally and figuratively. I just want to remember my son.

It's strange how memory works. Small things pop in your head, detached from meaning, floating like missing pieces you know belong to some big picture: I *do* know my son loved those banana-shaped cookies; he ate them with lots of drool, almost gnawing. I can see the spit sliding from his chubby face down his striped jumper: dark blue/light blue/dark blue/light blue/silver snaps. Or could this simply be memorized from the few photographs I managed to keep? Why are the only clothes I remember the ones in the pictures? Mine is such a selective nostalgia, my memory tangential. But as my life becomes more . . . I don't want to write about that either. I don't wanna write about myself, don't wanna write about his dad. I just wanna write about Greg.

And now it's not his birthday. And I'm in the airport being detected and inspected. Preparing to squeeze into a tight tube and scratch the sky. Just last week I told my students that the way things are today does not mean they've never been different. That there was a time when one could even carry water and wear shoes at the airport. Their surprise reminded me how our present moments can rewrite our histories. How maybe my son only remembers me for the me he sees and not the me I left behind, accidently or intentionally.

I can't even find the path back to my own past. I'm stuck going in circles in a cycle of spirals and loops. Sometimes, I have to break into my own memories to find some kind of map that guides me to the X marking the spot where the wishing goes away, where I remember not the years or the days but the moments with my dear, sweet boy.

But it's all trapped in fragments of breaking news, banana cookies, baby jumpers, and Polaroid pictures. The opposite of a trigger, whatever the word is that makes you want to remember . . .

When you can't.

Reading "adam thinking" by Lucille Clifton

What if we got it all wrong?
What if all this time, Eve was alone
and Adam had always been the devil?
What if Eve was the one who said *no*?
Why would we trust the word of a snake?

Survivor's Soliloquy:

Some girls say they wouldn't go down without a fight.
How they'd kick and scream, running into the night.
Don't tell anyone how weak you are. How quickly
you gave up, shut eyes tight. How your lips stitched
all by themselves. Save your breath for the run home.
Crawl back through an always ajar window. Sneak
frozen peas. Calm your swollen skin. Watch the ice
sweat to beads running down your thighs. Be quiet
when you cry. *Is it crying if you don't make a noise?*
Tuck yourself into a thin pair of sheets. Trace names
of crushes carved in your bedroom door with heavy,
wet eyes. Maybe the boys who say they love you
don't count. Count to 100. Count the hours until
sunrise. The time between breaths. The distance
between your back and the backdrop of the moon.
Ponder the number of dead stars your body could be.
Remember your first class is chemistry. Relive again
this night, when the smell of a dead guinea pig fills
a hole in your face, as you cut her tiny body to parts.

What do you do when you realize no one is coming to save you?

When my body forgets how to stand up for itself
I puddle, wallow, wash my spirit in a dark lake,
cocoon, lost inside myself, recreating someone
I do not yet know but believe in, listen to my past
selves see truth in things that do not spell them out,
see lies that used to look like hope, see all things
I thought the world was made of become a shadow
in the shape of me, look down for the first time,
and see my own two hands.

The Black
Woman Press
Conference

BJ Ruminates on Election Day (2016)

Who'd ever thought I'd live to see *this* mess?
    How we go from the first Black president
                to *this* shit?
Ain't no need to count them other votes.
  We already know what's gone happen.
           Same thing happen **every time**
they don't get they way—for once.
            Like when we had to have police
          just to go to school with them.
Or when we ain't have to sit
in the back of the bus no more.
        Why can't they ever let us be?
        Just hateful— No, it's jealousy;
         that's the truth about it.
Been *that* way all my life.
        Every time we try and do any kind of thing,
            Here. They. Go.
That's why they gave Obama such a hard time.
        Ain't wanna pass no laws,
      just wanted to make him look bad.
You know they wasn't gone let a smart,
good-looking Black man show them up.
      I seen it before: I remember when
      Harold Washington won and we was all so
      happy!
Went around like to cheer through the whole city.   **Ooowee!**

Everybody got on the bus saying good morning *that* day.
Everybody was wearing them buttons with his face on it.
Every Black person you walked by had a smile on they face.

White folks was **mad**.
    That's why they killed him.
    Talmbout he died . . . Shiiit!

                        A lie if I ever heard one.
Surprised they ain't take Obama out too.
    But you know Michelle ain't having *that*!
                      That's why he love her so.
Even though, I don't know
               what *that* feel like.
          I do wonder if   yo' body feel different
                  when a man love you right.
Yo' grandaddy was a dog.
         They all dogs   except Obama.
                  He different.
          He know how to love a Black woman.
Truth be told,
    that's probably why they hate him so.

On Being Mistaken for the Wrong Black Woman (Again)

Stuck in a room full of liberal white women
who cannot remember my name. Forget
everybody is wearing a name tag.

They keep calling me iterations
of someone they've mistaken
for a *Black friend*.

Keep calling me random women
(who don't look shit like me by the way).
Guess my face one of them inkblots

people project their fears upon,
making arbitrary meaning of what
they think they see.

These charity-donating, fake-coalition-
making "women" shout whatever
no-name Black face comes to mind.

I listen to speeches about oppression,
about "women" being paid eighty cents
of a [insert white] man's dollar

but when they say "women"
they don't mean me. They can't
even get my name right

let alone the calculation of
how much their not having *enough*
is tied to "women" like me having

nothing. For centuries, they chose
our positions, offering not even
a glass ceiling to go with the brooms

we used to sweep their floors.
Now, for the sake of the sex,
I am expected to forgive

to forget a past where my great-
grandmother would have been
made to eat the pie she baked

from a separate plate, in a separate
room emptied of white "women"
whose kitchens she cleaned

while being called everything,
except her name.

Etiquette

Good women should rise with the sun,
Cook a hot meal or at least a pot of grits.
Your kitchen is filled with the smell
Of cracked chicken shells, stale grease.

You pretend to care in company,
Eat packaged food on paper plates
When the judge and jury leave.
People speak of checking in on you.

You think of homemade chicken soup.
They think of finding you a man,
One with steel-toe boots and a hammer.
They ask why you don't long for the fit:

A white dress, a name that sounds
No better than your daddy's gift.
You want to be uncouth. You want
What they say doesn't belong to you.

Professional Development

Stuff into your panties these objects and pretend
When the time comes, you'll be ready to lie.

Raise your hand!   Say you can!

    Even if you can't yet.

Nobody knows what the fuck they're doing
Anyhow.
              Join the club.

Don't let a man give you the sun
For the gorgeous, lonely moon.

In exchange,
    You will only be mystery,
    No more than a howl in the night.

Give back the sky and scratch his eyes out,
Call the pain democracy.

Be more than a magic spell.
        Be real.

Undreamt
Manifested fucking destiny!

They say,
"Men are willing to take the necessary risks. . . ."

Why let them have all the evil,
Be all the greedy and neglect?

Look at you!
            You are free to be as selfish
            As you want to be.

That's the key!

See, you too are genius.
Yes, you too can rule the world.

After all, you helped form it
In the choking of a man's hard dick.

So, why should you clear the way?
Are you not the persuasion
Commanding it to stand and stay?

Salute yourself!
Understand that power does not ask
Nor permit.

You must snatch away their weak sacks
And pin them to your lips.

Pull their kingdom to shriveling collapse.

Dear Everybody Who Ain't a Black Woman

We ain't going nowhere.
We cannot be wished away
Or washed away or replaced.
We are the mold and the model
The starshine and the clay.
The deep stories of the dirt
The earth heaped upon the bones
And the bones, and the feet above.
We the hands working the soil
Stirring the pot, offering breast
Wearing the hell outta that dress
Or blue jeans or even nothing at all.
Yeah, sometimes we a hot mess
But sometimes we be working that suit
And running that company,
Teaching that class,
Leading the chorus,
Walking them streets,
Pacing that prison floor,
Haunting your towns
After you gun us down
And forget to say our names.
I want you to say my name:
Recite me, write me down
Should you ever find me gone,
If I never come up for air,
If I leave gently in my sleep

Or by accident
Or by my own hands
     —Or yours—
Know that I had a name.
That I was born, had body, had love.
I had fury, had family, had dreams
Had fears and lived fearlessly: I lived.
I was human. I was flawed and flawless.
I was the whole and half-truth at once.
I was.   I am.   We are.

Just when I thought I was grown, I grew

Beyond bowed back and bent knee,
    I am more than glorified suffering
draped in silence and modesty.
    Bigger than the promise of a good
life in some white God's eternity.
    My existence deserves more than
makeshift morality. My survival
    is not symbolic of a Samaritan's
noble deeds. I am neither servant
    nor vessel to be used and emptied,
not a trophy rescued from the trash.
    These scars are not metaphors
for mythical birds surviving the fire,
    their singed wings escaping ash.
I am a creation of vast, glorious
    shaping. And I am learning
to breathe, to be a cloud circling
    skies of clarity. I am new
beginnings. I am April. I am spring
    rain and remnants. The release
that nurtures the seed. And I am
    the green spawning from dirt
to yellow feed for honeybees.
    I am multiplicity growing
possibility, and nothing can stop this
    flowering.

Conjure
Woman

I'm a Woman

after Koko Taylor

You gift my girlish grin hot whiskey
Golden brown juke-joint fire on tongue

You bring out the Mississippi in me
Light my cigar, baby, you *is* my match

I am your way, your truth, the light
I am goddamn sky cracked open

Your thunder rolling in the deep
You live 'tween the gap in my thighs

So big in yo' eyes, I be a planet
A galaxy for you to wonder at

Yo' wild brown lady friend
Yo' Jack Daniel champion

Drankin' any man in reach
Under the whole damn table

You cross The Delta in me
Swamping yo' body 'n' soul

I be yo' heaven, yo' sweet hell
Sugar, I put a spell on you

This voodoo coochie be the Yazoo
Washing away all yo' Weary Blues

She Had Some Husbands

after Joy Harjo

she had some husbands made
of rocks and glass
    some like keys fallen
    from trees in tailspins
husbands who grew
like sponges in the rain
    scrubbing her face to
    see if she bled the same
she had some husbands
a dozen a million
    a planet of bad men
    chained inside her gut
she had them all
had husbands
    who had no wives
    who had no lives
who grew from dirt
who dropped like flies
    splat husbands
    on bottoms of shoes
on backs of spoons
streaking her tongue
    with the residue
    of husbands won
until she had one

until she had none
    left husbands who were
    never hers to begin
left them all begging
to be more than kept men

Mirror, Mirror on the Ceiling

seeing himself in her   never she   for she   never is
        never real   to begin
a deep grave   she is to him   an open flesh
      to pour into   his pain   his hurt
his dirt   until she becomes the cut
    her face   the festering sore
her eyes   the sin that won't shut   her skin
    the scab   unfolding   her body
his wound   that won't heal a dead man
    confused   her mind   for his tomb
her heart for his rot
          fisted like an apple
     bitten then
          dropped.
dropped
    then bitten
          fisted like an apple
her rot   his heart
    her tomb   his mind   confused
a dead man   won't heal   her wound
    his body unfolding   the scab
his skin   won't shut   the sin
    his eyes   sore   festering

his face   the cut   he becomes
          her dirt   her hurt
her pain   to pour into   an open flesh
    to her   he is   a deep grave
to begin   seeing herself in him

Things to Do in the Belly of a Whale

after Dan Albergotti

·

light a candle. set it in the hole of a tooth.
lay a feather on the tongue bed. fill a glass
with saliva, for there is no fresh water here.

call the dead for answers. only they know
the way in and out of the belly of a beast,
only they know this is a beast and not a whale.

a once man walking the earth until cursed
and cast into the sea, becoming a swollen
thing with no legs, no arms, no hands
to choke me.

but a mouth, big as a city, built for one,
swallowed whole woman, fooled
by the beauty of blue waves crashing
against the edge of a sea.

freely, I walked into his parted lips,
a door welcoming me home,
but a house is not a home
and a room is not a house
and a chair is not a room.

this is a cage: built with the bones
of women before me, their ribs his ribs,
my body to be the jugular notch.

the dead don't speak. they answer back,
call in the voice of my grandmother
midday and say, *run child.*

but I cannot run,
can only hide
here in this dark cavity.

the creatures outside swim by and say
the way out of the whale is forgiveness,
that I must offer it in exchange for escape.

but the beast never begged, *forgive me,*
and had he, I would have cried, *No!*

so, I stay stuck in his belly
until I kick the candle over
and make a hell of everything inside.

Run

As fast and far as you can
    from a man who turns
more monster than man
    every time you look back
                on your heels
        his claws
            on your back
        his teeth
                tail whipping the wind
                 like a scorpion searching
             for the softest part of flesh
don't stop where the trees stop
        even if the night holds your breath
thickets swell with your blood
        and the wolf howls
           picking your skin between the bones
let the dark swallow your lungs
  let the branches slash your face
        shards of stone crack your feet

        the moon is your light
           let *away* be your direction.

The Graveyard Feasts on Fools

like a loose thread
in a stitched hem
    unraveling
with each effort
to mend
    dead skin
to body like a ball
    of yarn
unbecoming bones
tossed and thrown
    cursed ashes
to dust, to gone
    to ghost
to grief, to loss
    too lost,
you fool,
    you lost.

Incubus Is Latin for Fuckboy

I never lost a man I loved   too much   to death   to the dirt
but I lost you   because you didn't want to be found   out
my life   you went   and "got free"   on a Tuesday afternoon
claimed to be   long gone   lost   to some other dimension
where you were not a demon   but a god.

I knew nothing of your divination
                 mortals like me don't deserve a word
if I were a prophet like my daddy
                 maybe I would've known
you were the Second Coming of Christ
                 maybe I would have bowed down
would have washed, with my hair, your feet
                 maybe that would have kept you.

the dinner went uneaten   after you   chewed   my heart out
                 what was left to stomach?
grease crept into the chicken swimming the pan
                 the flour skin slid away
the way dead things fall off the bone.

I woke up in an empty room   full of shit   belonging to you.

the groceries I bought for your palate went bad
                 when I drove the kids for takeout
                 I almost called to ask your order
                 but you changed your number

and I don't even know where the fuck you are . . .

Fuckboy!

I threw it all out: *the food, the table, the pots, the couch,*
  your shoes, them lies, yo' ugly ass ties,
  the photos, the mirrors . . . the sheets
  that smelled of you.

you are a missing person   who if found would be
      alive and well   running in place   pretending
yo' raggedy feet never trampled so much as a cockroach.

who knew those stories of men going for a pack of smokes,
never returning, could be true?

you left as would any empty man: cheap guitar on your back
my last dollar   my suitcase   (yet to be returned)

life stuffed into a checked bag
              thinking *you* somebody's idea of the Blues . . .
                    'cept *you ain't*
                          no John Lee Hooker
                    you ain't
                          no Howlin' Wolf
                    you ain't
                          no B.B. King
                    you ain't even
                          my granddaddy n'em.

you a Fuckboy:
          English for Incubus
          a ghost, a myth

an ain't shit Negro
who wasn't raised right

& I'm glad yo' ass is gone: I been saved from the depths of hell

set free from a lie I didn't know I was living   praise de lawd!

I don't wanna be angry.   I don't wanna be sad.
               I wanna be bad,
                         like Jesse James
wanna disappear you   wanna do my own dirty work
               cuz I'm the big boss.
so, in my dreams   I take you down to the river
               I gut yo' body like a fish   you die.
I bring you back to life;   I kill you again   'til I bury
               this memory   & fill this wide-open hole
                       in my heart   with *my* heart.

Premature
Elegies

Why Moondust Smells Like Spent Gunpowder

Some nights the black sky is the only black thing left
breathing, as we are left holding our bereft breath
straining at spent gunpowder in smoky streetlights
squinting until the *boom!* looks like confetti moon;
we gawk like dragonflies in every direction
at somebody's child flying like a sliver of glitter
sucked to black clouds inhaling black bodies
burning like shooting constellations escaping:
what curious ghosts! Oblique, thunderous arrows
fresh flares of fire in flight fleeing this blue-green
gobbling planet to mausoleums on the moon,
where Whitey can no longer hide from us in peace.

Morphology

Studies say the earliest language was pictorial, like horses drawn in ancient caves. Though evolved, our words have yet to lose sight. Some words grow into others, supplanting suffixes, until letters seem distant enough to mean a new thing, except nothing is new, and definitions belong, as Morrison says, to the definers.

My ancestors passed along messages without saying a word, warned of figures dressed in blue, grimaced behind a gun, a dog, a fire hose, all but the fire-wielding hand shown beneath a white sheet, burning property for the audacity of a people to be property no more, until that last ember strewn itself across a black night, leaving only memories for coming generations to scribe.

I recollect a scene, crossing a busy street outside Chicago, running an errand, a pack of Black girls becoming stuck in the middle of the road as a carload of white men made us play a twisted game of chicken, circling the median, shouting, *"Niggers!"* until we shrieked and cried. An ugly stain on a string of fun '90s summer days. Decades later and I'm still stuck with the ghosts of white boys having fun. Still see the grocery store, an Aldi, with a pay phone, change for candy spent instead on a call home for help.

Generations have come and gone, and we still have to hear white people pretend the word "Nigger" fell from someone else's sky. The one credit they will deny. A creation of strung letters forming a new word, abstract 'til cursed with meaning, concrete as a city block where the decomposed lie center of news compositions, like "Black-on-Black crime," enough times to forget it is a term grown from shock at the loss of a past time where white folks could pick which "Nigger" to split with a little six-letter lie.

Run, Run, Go Away

(an anti-lullaby)

A silhouette threat
to someone else's good day
turns everything black
to something in the water
menace ready to bite back

Black boy plays with toy
in park, Black man shops for toy
in Walmart, ring round
brown ones, pockets full of ash
to ashes, only we fall

An unraveling echo
moving faster the further
reaching with arms tied
becoming magic
when you never knew juju

Black girl sleeps in peace
at home, Black woman follows
a dream job alone,
rain or shine, rest or wake, dust
to dirt, death reincarnate

"Keep Him Here"
for Todd

I saw your eyes today, the dark brown bottom
half-moons swimming in a sea of skin and fight

You might not make it to see yourself born
from seed, so I will tell you stories

What your kids would look like, how they'd laugh,
cackling as you do, dancing with no rhythm too

Small bodies formed from her pale bony mound
whispering, *please*, running back to these wires when

Time begins again. Time begins
again. Time begins again.

You will never know
how she loves you if you go away—stay

For your brother, who'll learn stiff hairs on a back
can speak even on an ocean's bottom, even in

Someone else's war, he would swim through
ten thousand dark waves, for you to—stay

Don't you loosen a toe from the dirt to the air,
don't you fly to a god you thought you knew

Your mother would lasso her shrinking body
to your ankle bone, melt to black sky with you

Leaving the ground a broken shell of creamy
skin and rouge

buckling face, her eyes sinking at the sight,
the bruise of you, the jigsaw bones

Even if the breath is not all yours, tell us
you will find your way home.

Elegy for the Cough Drop Man

for Grandpa Gibson

You lived, surrounded by used books
plucked from Salvation Army bins,
jars filled with half-dollar coins,
old newspapers packed the corners
of your coach house home, one modest
television set to public access droning
WTTW: "your window to the world,"
your tallest granddaughter, who lived
below you, found you—eventually,
escaped blood thickened, your hand
eternally gripping a shower curtain
ripped in the fall; I imagine you went
away in that same blue robe from '92
when you lived, in that apartment,
and I visited on Easter, *remember*?
I want you to remember me that way
—all ruffle and lace, and I will try to
forget the robe and think of your red,
round-cheeked half smile beneath
round-corner glasses, wearing that
same white shirt with a new bolo tie,
the two long strings pulled too close
to the collar, a lasso around your neck
squeezing that soft, whispery chuckle,
tickling your thick mustache that always
smelled of mint, your pockets always
filled with gifts of sweet vapor.

Keepsake

Folded in a Ziploc bag, tucked in a box somewhere in my bedroom, are the letters and artifacts from people who loved me who are no longer here. Though they've passed on, I write back to them in my poems. Like my grandpa who, on the few occasions we conversed, spoke of the sky's beauty and color and God and something about the importance of awe, as I sat quietly in the backseat of his Deuce and a Quarter with the windows rolled down. All I remember between those random weekends spent at Old Country Buffet, The Salvation Army, and the dollar show is how important he thought it was for me to look up at the clouds every now and then.

The only inheritance I have from him is that small advice remarking the blue masterpiece above, and a news article clipped from a local paper around the year 2000 that reads: "Abbot testing arthritis drug for kids, Crohn's." He bracketed the paragraph with information on clinical trials for D2E7 before placing it in an envelope and passing it on to my aunt, who passed it on to me; on the front is his handwriting: *concerning April*, my name circled in black ink, now smeared more than twenty years later, the envelope still folded inside the bag, inside the box.

I first held on to this keepsake for sentimental value, but later realized that D2E7 would become Humira, which I began injecting into my abdomen ten years after he sent the article to me. I wonder if things could have turned out differently had I not waited so long, had I listened to what Grandpa was trying to say all those years ago. Though we weren't close, he was family, even if there are no memories of him comforting me in times of pain or visiting me in a hospital. He left me with the lesson that sometimes people can say, "I love you" even if they don't *say* it at all.

She had some grief

she had some grief and called it Holy
she had some grief and it called her
every day of the week

she had some grief and shared it
with no one except the little voice
inside her head

'til one day the little voice said
let there be night
~~forever~~

Teratology

Trauma lives in your memory like a phantom
    limb left after the severing; the dark
velvet covers your eyes, and you feel
    its fingernails float across your skin
threatening to claw if you peek; if you
    speak its name, it might come; remember
monsters live by invitation, and if it comes
    you might listen; remember, sympathy
is a trap, and now you are trapped: a dumbstruck
    doe stuck in the middle of the road
mistaking freight trains for screams, blown tires
    for weeping; when you open your eyes
you don't see it anymore, only a mouth seething;
    you look around, you look down
you pick the shards of mirror from your bloodied fists.

[Failed] Abecedarian

A city far away and settled
Beneath the Northern sky

    Crawl to the cracked window
    Down ten-stories high—I see

        Enough life to consider my
        Face is not a pair of wings
        God blows and wishes for an ear
Hear my grandma's distant plea
Inches before both ready feet
Jump high enough to fly
—Keel this blue musing
        Leave no runny yolk
        Messy down the sides
        Now, be a girl again, stirring
        Over a bowl of cracked yellow
Pulling out the white specks, floating

    Quicker than a whisper leaves a lie
    Return to water what can't be held
    Silently, become the spun eye of a sea

        Then part it red and pray
        Until the gray goes away
        Vanishing to a hollow

Wind circling back again
X-iting this dark space—leave

Yearning for the light

Zero in, turn: there is an open door.

Afterlife

My daddy had a gift
he used for dominion
over all things
he began a powerless man
but grew mighty, to some
they say train a child
in the way
then I parted ways
with Black Jesus
to believe in a world I own
where origin lives in a house
brushed with red-dirt water
and the smell of cows
I never milked

In this house
there are women with palms
big enough to swallow fists
their raised hairs tremble
the fingers of god conjure
grandmothers' dead
grandmothers into the soul
of my unborn child
from the dry birth
before my birth

on a couch in Mississippi
     we push
history through space
     in time, we all return

Epilogue

My son, at five, tells me how the world began

"the Earth started as a seed
then bounced off the sun
rolled around in space &
growed & growed &
growed until
there were birds
& squirrels
& grass & grass
no concretes, just grass
& grass."

Acknowledgments

I thank God for my life's story—the joy and the sorrow, the victory and the fight, and the peace I have made with it all.

The utmost gratitude to my sons who have spent their lives making stories with me, who teach me to see the world differently. I would not be the writer I am without my boys. Gregory and Jaylin, you are my greatest poem.

To those who never wrote a poem, but showed me how to tell a story—Grandma Bobbie's lessons, Kool Daddy's blues, Mama Pam's manifestos, Daddy Grant's sermons of "good news," Twyla and Pam's sisterly reflections, Mally and BG's brotherly anecdotes, and the chronicles of many loved ones—these are your stories too. Love to all my family for supporting and inspiring me on and off the page.

An abundance of gratitude to Dr. Kelly Norman Ellis; you saw beauty in my words thirteen years ago and did not let me put down my pen. Immense gratitude to the numerous friends and writers who have supported my work, from the writing community in Chicago that shaped me to the Twin Cities writing community that is my second home. To the many who have read, workshopped, talked me through, celebrated, or shared with me along this path, I cannot describe how grateful I am.

Thank you to the institutions and organizations that have provided me space or resources to grow as a writer over the years: Chicago State University's MFA program (best cohort ever), where it all began, The Loft Literary Center Mentor Series (my amazing cohort), Vermont Studio Center, Callaloo Creative

Writing Workshop, VONA Writing Workshop (dopest workshop group), Watering Hole Poetry Retreat, Tin House Winter Workshop, The Sustainable Arts Foundation, Write On, Door County, and any others.

Publishing this book with Amistad Press would not have happened without Randall Horton, who, from the start, has pushed me to share my writing with the world, and Jennifer Baker, who received and believed in my manuscript. I am immensely grateful to you both. And to my editor Francesca Walker, thank you for carrying on the work to become more than what I imagined it could be. I am beyond appreciative to everyone at Amistad involved in bringing this book to life.

And thank you, dear reader, for joining me on this journey.

Sincere acknowledgments to the following publications where various versions of these poems first appeared:

Obsidian: Literature & Arts in the African Diaspora—"Ruins"

Crazyhorse—"Ghazal for a fast black girl gazing from a locked window" and "Vestiges"

RHINO Poetry—"Superstar"

Michigan Quarterly Review—"3X5 Ekphrasis of a Past Life"

Green Mountains Review—"Blue Magic"

Naugatuck River Review—"Keep Him Here" and "On Being Mistaken for the Wrong Black Woman, Again"

The Kenyon Review—"Things to Do in the Belly of a Whale"

Prairie Schooner—"Neighborhood Watch II"

Water~Stone Review—"Coldwater"

PANK—"Dawn," "Recessive," and "Transgression"

Valley Voices—"Etiquette" and "Professional Development"

Pluck! Journal of Affrilachian Arts—"Afterlife"

Off the Charts: The American Journal of Nursing—"How to survive holding your breath"

AsUs Journal—"Baptism"

"The Draping of Broods," "Tete-a-tete," and "Domesticated" appear in my chapbook *Automation* (Willow Books, 2015).

About the Author

April Gibson is a poet, writer, and professor from the South Side of Chicago. Her work has appeared in the *Kenyon Review*, *Michigan Quarterly Review*, *RHINO Poetry*, *Prairie Schooner*, and elsewhere. Gibson is a recipient of the Gwendolyn Brooks Poetry Award among other honors. She teaches English at Malcolm X College in Chicago.